# BLACKJACK BAILOUT II

## AN IMPROVED WINNER

**Learn exactly when to:**
Quit after reaching a Win Goal.
Quit a Losing Run

### RAY FRANKE

**EXPRESSO**

Executive Center 777, Dunsmuir Street Vancouver, BC V71K4
1-888-721-0662 ext 101
info@expressopublishing.com

# DEDICATION

To my recently deceased wife, Kay, for her patience with me spending days on end writing this book.

To my good friend, Norm, for his field testing and collaboration about blackjack over the years.

To those authors of websites and books referenced herein for their contributions to the body of blackjack knowledge.

And, finally to Microsoft for its Excel spreadsheet, without which this book would not have been possible.

# TABLE OF CONTENTS

# PREVIEW

This book is in the category of "Win without Card Counting" blackjack books.

Like other books in the category, this book contradicts conventional wisdom that the only winning blackjack system involves "card counting".

Different from other books in the category, this book offers "proof" of winning in the long run.

With apologies to Kenny Roger's "The Gambler", the following parody describes what a blackjack player needs to know and do to be a winner, on average, in the long run.

- You got to know how to play 'em. ♫
- Know how to bet 'em.
- ***Know when to walk away.***
- Know when to stay.
- ***Keep track of your system.***
- While playin' at the table.
- ***It tells when to be quittin'***
- Before the deal is done. ♫

In its entirety, the parody describes a blackjack "system", consisting of the 3 basic "strategies":

1. Basic Playing Strategy (Hit, Stand, Double Down, Split a Pair).
2. Betting Strategies (Flat and Progression betting).
3. Bailout Strategy (Set a Win Goal & Limit losses).

The following chapter titles include a summary of the content.

<u>Basic Playing Strategy</u>. There are over 500 different combinations of the player's initially dealt 2-card hand and the dealer's up-card.

Fortunately, others have developed a simple "cheat sheet" that shows the best play to make for each of the combinations. Most dealers all0w a player to use it at the table.

My version, a "crib card", is displayed in the chapter.

<u>Proof Testing</u> The chapter describes how an "Excel®" spreadsheet was used to prove and compare long run results of different "Win without Card Counting" bet/bailout strategies.

<u>Bet Strategy</u>. Different bet strategies are selected, all to be used at a $10 minimum bet table, but scalable to other size minimum bets.

1. <u>$10 flat betting</u>. This is basically for reference and comparison to progression betting.

2. <u>Positive Progressions</u>. Increase the bet after a winning hand. Flat bet $10 after a losing hand.
3. <u>Negative Progressions</u>. Increase the bet after a losing hand. Flat bet $10 after a winning hand.

All are proof tested for long run results using the Excel® spreadsheet. All are first tested for results without using a bailout strategy for later comparison of results after being combined with a bailout strategy.

<u>Bailout Strategy</u>. This chapter reveals how a relatively simple bailout strategy can be combined with each of the different bet strategies to obtain the best long run results.

<u>Bet/Bailout Combinations</u>. The bet strategies, after each is combined with its best bailout strategy, are proof tested for long range results, again using the Excel® spreadsheet.

<u>Case the Table (Retracted)</u>. For LP bettors only. A previous edition of this book presupposes a change in routine will significantly increase your average long-run winnings.

Upon a detailed check, it was found that it does not. My apologies for the previous error.

<u>The Bailout Advantage</u>. This is simply a list comparing the results of the bet strategies with "no bailout" and then when combined with "full bailout" strategies.

<u>Simple Trac</u>. A "How to" guide to track the excess of losing hands over winners and also after reaching a Win Goal (WG).

<u>Track the Running Total</u>. To know your own personal long run results.

<u>Scaling Up the Bet Level</u>. Changing the bet/bailout strategies and long run results for other than $10 minimum bet tables.

<u>Recap</u>. Speaks for itself.

I hope to have achieved a goal to "KISS" (Keep It Simple, Stupid). More simple, more fun.

# BASIC PLAYING STRATEGY

This chapter describes the decision (stand, hit, double down or split a pair) a player needs to make on each hand for the best results, long run.

There are over 500 possible combinations of a player's original 2-card hand and the dealer's up-card requiring a playing decision.

The best playing decision is independent of the size of the bet riding on the hand.

Basic playing strategy was first determined mathematically by the "4 Horsemen of Blackjack", Baldwin, Cantley, Maisel & McDermott. They published a book describing the strategy, entitled "Playing Blackjack to Win", 1957.

The strategy is kept up to date by Michael Shackleford, the "Wizard of Odds", on his website (highly recommended).

It is applicable to the table setup and rules of play like those used by most casinos today:

- Use of a 6-deck shoe with a "cut card".

- Dealer stands on any 17.
- Pays 3:2 for a natural blackjack.
- Player may double down on any 2-card hand.
- May split any pair up to 2 hands. (Usual rule is 4)
- May double down on any split pair hand, except A's.
- Table offers "insurance" but is never taken.
- "Surrender" option, if offered, is not taken.

Basic playing strategy is described by the "Wizard" and others, on various arrangements of rows and columns on a matrix chart, often referred to as a "cheat sheet".

I call my arrangement a "crib card", which can be folded from top to bottom into credit card size, making it easy to carry and use at the actual blackjack table.

| BASIC PLAYING STRATEGY | | | | | | | | | | | | |
|---|---|---|---|---|---|---|---|---|---|---|---|---|
| | | ——— Dealer Up-Card ——— | | | | | | | | | | |
| Playr Hand | | 2 | 3 | 4 | 5 | 6 | 7 | 8 | 9 | 10 | A | |
| H | 5-8 | Always Hit | | | | | | | | | | |
| a | 9 | Hit | Dbl Dwn | | | | Hit | | | | | |
| r | 10 | Dbl Dwn | | | | | | | | Hit | | |
| d | 11 | Dbl Dwn | | | | | | | | | Hit | |
| | 12 | Hit | | Stand | | | Hit | | | | | |
| | 13-16 | Stand | | | | | Hit | | | | | |
| | 17-21 | Always Stand | | | | | | | | | | |
| S | A,8-10 | Always Stand | | | | | | | | | | |
| o | A,2-3 | Hit | | | DD | | Hit | | | | | |
| f | A,4-5 | Hit | | Dbl Dwn | | | Hit | | | | | |
| t | A,6 | Hit | Dbl Dwn | | | | Hit | | | | | |
| | A,7 | Std | Dbl Dwn | | | | Stand | | Hit | | | |
| | | 2 | 3 | 4 | 5 | 6 | 7 | 8 | 9 | 10 | A | |
| P | 2's,3's, | Split | | | | | Hit | | | | | |
| a | 4's | Hit | | Split | | | Hit | | | | | |
| i | 5's | Dbl Dwn | | | | | | | | Hit | | |
| r | 6's | Split | | | | | Hit | | | | | |
| s | 7's | Split | | | | | Hit | | | | | |
| | 8's, A's | Always Split | | | | | | | | | | |
| | 9's | Split | | | | | Std | Split | | Stand | | |
| | 10's | Always Stand | | | | | | | | | | |

Use the card by finding your hand in a row down the left column and then crossing over to the right to find the column headed by the dealer's up-card. The intersection displays the play to make for best results in the long run.

A copy of this card is displayed on the last page of this book, free to be cut out and used at the blackjack table, when the dealer permits.

Also, refer to the crib card while practicing blackjack on your computer. The more you practice, the less often you will need to refer to your crib card at the blackjack table because you have committed more plays to memory.

A recommended computer program to use for practice is wizardofodds.com/play/blackjack/.

An example of an often-misplayed 2-card hand is player holding a hard 16 and the dealer up-card is a 7 through A.

Most players in this situation seem to hesitate and then choose to "stand".

The crib card recommendation for the best play is "hit".

The situation is a loser most of the time, no matter what choice is made but the math experts have proved you will *lose less* in the long run if you hit.

Another example of a misplayed hand is when player holds a soft 18 (A,7) and the dealer up-card is a 3, 4, 5, or 6.

It seems most players in this situation choose to stand as an 18 hand.

Basic playing strategy says the best play is to "double down".

The situation is a winner most of the time, no matter what choice is made, but the math experts have proven you will *win more* in the long run if you double down.

Overall conclusion: Using basic playing strategy is the most important "**must do**" rule of playing blackjack.

# PROOF TESTING

Different than all the other "Win without Card Counting" books on the market, this book presents "_proof_" of the long run winning results of the bet/bailout strategies described herein.

The first user of a computer to prove a blackjack winner was Dr. Edward O. Thorpe, author of "Beat the Dealer©". He made many runs of approximately 1,000,000 hands of blackjack to discover and _proof test_ the card counting bet system to be a long run winner.

Currently, there are several 1,000,000 hand simulation programs on the market that can be used to proof test any bet strategy described to it.

Unfortunately, they do not provide a way to describe a bailout strategy, making them unusable for proof testing the bet/bailout strategies in this book.

So, I created a different proof testing program using an Excel® computer spreadsheet, to record the results, split screen, of playing 31,658 hands of computer blackjack.

A portion of the spreadsheet is illustrated, next page.

## 31,658 Hand Spreadsheet

| T | U | V | W | X | Y |
|---|---|---|---|---|---|
| If new shoe (n) | If Splt Pair (s) | If Dbl Dwn (d) | Init Bet ($) | Act'l Bet ($) | Rslt of hnd |
| n |  |  | 10 | 10 | l |
|  |  |  | 20 | 20 | w |
|  |  |  | 10 | 10 | l |
|  |  |  | 20 | 20 | w |
|  |  |  | 10 | 10 | l |
|  |  |  | 20 | 20 | w |
|  |  |  | 10 | 10 | l |
|  |  |  | 20 | 20 | w |
|  |  |  | 10 | 10 | l |
|  |  |  | 20 | 20 | l |
|  |  |  | 40 | 40 | l |
|  |  |  | 45 | 45 | p |
|  |  |  | 45 | 45 | w |
|  |  |  | 10 | 10 | l |
|  |  |  | 20 | 20 | w |
|  | s |  | 10 | 10 | w |
|  | s |  | 10 | 10 | l |
|  |  |  | 20 | 20 | w |
|  |  |  | 10 | 10 | w |
|  |  | d | 10 | 20 | dp |
| n |  |  | 10 | 10 | l |

I loaded the spreadsheet in separate columns, and row by row, with:

1. "n", if the start of a new shoe (column "T").
2. "s", if a split pair hand (column "U".
3. "d" if a double-down hand (column "V").
4. The "Result of hand" (column "Y").

It was then programmed to accept a description of a bet/bailout strategy and report the result for the run.

The 31,658-hand run is considered a legitimate "long run" test platform because it's "% loss of the amount bet" is within the margin of error of the result mathematicians calculated for a million-hand run of flat bet blackjack hands.

For flat betting, no bailout strategy, the average loss was 0.48 % of the amount bet (4.8 cents per $10 bet). This is often referred to as the built-in "house edge".

The main advantages of the spreadsheet program compared to the 1,000,000-hand blackjack simulation programs on the market are:

- It uses the **_same_** run of 31,658 hands to show results of various bet/bailout strategies tested. This eliminates any margin of error when comparing results. The 1,000,000-hand simulation programs use a different run for each bet strategy test, resulting in a margin of error, albeit very small.

- By using the same run, a proof test result is revealed in a matter of seconds, rather than many minutes/hours required for the million-hand simulation programs to make a new run.

A section of the spreadsheet allows entry of a description of the bet strategy to be proof tested. It's a "fill in the yellow blocks" section as illustrated for $10 flat betting.

**SETUP:**

| Min Bet Table $ | 10 | | | | | | | | | | | | |
|---|---|---|---|---|---|---|---|---|---|---|---|---|---|
| Buy-in$ | ?? | | | | | | | | | | | | |
| Bet Line(BL)$ | ?? | | | | | | | | | | | | |

**BET STRATEGY:**

| Start Bet$ | 10 | | | | | | | | | | | | |
|---|---|---|---|---|---|---|---|---|---|---|---|---|---|

Bet Sequences: Based on a Winning streak, ignoring pushes.

| Streak of W Hands | 1 | 2 | 3 | 4 | 5 | 6 | 7 | 8 | 9 | 10 | 11 | | |
|---|---|---|---|---|---|---|---|---|---|---|---|---|---|
| Bet after Streak $ | 10 | 10 | 10 | 10 | 10 | 10 | 10 | 10 | 10 | 10 | 10 | | |

Based on a Losing streak, ignoring pushes.

| Streak of L Hands | -1 | -2 | -3 | -4 | -5 | -6 | -7 | -8 | -9 | -10 | -11 | -12 | -13 |
|---|---|---|---|---|---|---|---|---|---|---|---|---|---|
| Bet after Streak $ | 10 | 10 | 10 | 10 | 10 | 10 | 10 | 10 | 10 | 10 | 10 | 10 | 10 |

The specific "Buy-in" and "Bet line (BL)" $$ will be revealed in a later chapter because they vary depending on the chosen bet strategy.

The BL $$ are set up to supply chips for placing bets.

The buy-in $$ is always larger than the BL $$. The difference is set aside in a "slush fund" (explained later).

The "start bet" square is filled in with the minimum bet listed for the table (Ex: 10 at a $10 table).

The longest winning run streak per shoe without a losing hand was 11 hands in the 31,658-hand spreadsheet. So, if betting $10 flat, all 11 squares would be filled in with the #10, as illustrated, previous page.

Likewise, the longest losing run streak per shoe without a winning hand in the spreadsheet was 13 hands. So, if betting $10 flat, all 13 squares would also be filled in with the #10.

If proof testing a progression bet strategy, all 11 squares in the winning row and all 13 squares in the losing row still need to be filled in (numbers different than $10 flat bet).

Moving on, the following illustration shows the bailout strategy p0rtion of the setup with the yellow square filled in with "4", describing the bailout strategy that gave the best long run results when combined with the $10 flat bet strategy.

| **BAILOUT STRATEGY** (ignoring pushes), Bailout if: | | |
| --- | --- | --- |
| LOSING hands exceed Winning hands----by [ 4 ] | Reaching a Win Goal (WG) of: $ [ 40 ] | |

Unfortunately, this is not a "one size fits all" bailout strategy. The "4" changes to a "5" for many other bet strategies and the "40" could be any other size.

So, to find the best result, both 4 and 5 were "cut and tried" using the 31,658-hand spreadsheet.

The "Results" of each step-by-step test is displayed in an area directly below the bailout strategy.

The following example shows the best results found for $10 flat betting combined with its optimum bailout strategy.

**BAILOUT STRATEGY** (ignoring pushes), Bailout if:

LOSING hands exceed Winning hands--by | 4 | Reaching a Win Goal (WG) of: $ | 40 |

**RESULTS**:

| Overall $$ Stats————▶ | Avg Bet Size$ | | $ Bet | | $ W/L | %W/L |
|---|---|---|---|---|---|---|
| | 10.92 | | 205250 | | 975 | 0.48 |

| Session Stats ▶ | # Played | # Won | % Won | Avg W/L $ | Max Win $ | Max Loss $ |
|---|---|---|---|---|---|---|
| | 1428 | 537 | 37.61 | 0.68 | 135 | -50 |

| Number of shoes = | | 1848 |
|---|---|---|

| All HANDS (Detail): | | | | SPLIT PAIR HANDS (Detail): | | | |
|---|---|---|---|---|---|---|---|
| Type | # Played | # Won | % Won | Type | # Played | # Won | % Won |
| Hit/Stand | 14764 | 6455 | 43.7 | Hit/Stand | 618 | 305 | 49.4 |
| DD | 1606 | 968 | 60.3 | DD | 90 | 62 | 68.9 |
| BW | 861 | 861 | 100.0 | Pushes | 54 | | |
| Pushes | 1561 | 0 | 0 | Total | 762 | 367 | 48.2 |
| Total | 18792 | 8284 | | | | | |

| Type | # | % of Totl |
|---|---|---|
| Won | 8284 | 44.08 |
| Lost | 8947 | 47.61 |
| Push | 1561 | 8.31 |

If interested in obtaining a copy of the spreadsheet for your personal use, email the author at:

rkfranke@bellsouth.net

# BET STRATEGY

It has been reported that 23 different versions of card counting bet strategies have been published, all _proven_ long run winners.

It seemed reasonable to assume there could also be several "Progression" bet strategies that win, long run.

Results of the betting strategies presented in this chapter are based on playing at a $10 minimum bet table without a bailout strategy being employed (no bailout).

Also, all bet strategies are proof tested for long run results using the 31,658-hand spreadsheet.

**Flat betting.** The long run result was a loss of a little less than ½ of 1 % of the amount bet (-0.481 %, to be precise).

This is an average loss of only 4.81 cents for every $10 bet.

**<u>Win-hand Progressions (WP)</u>**. These are positive progressions that:

- Increase the bet after a winning hand.
- Bet table minimum after a losing hand.

This is a "feel good" bet strategy because, after a winning hand, the next bet placed includes "house money" just received in the payoff rather than using up more money from your buy-in.

If letting your original bet plus the payoff ride for the next bet, it's either referred to as a "Double-up" or a "Parlay" bet strategy.

But there is a real limit to the number of times in a row a player can "parlay" bets. This is the "max bet limit", posted on the blackjack table.

For example, at a $10 table, the max bet limit is typically $1000. A "parlayed" WP bet strategy would be:

WP=20,40,80,160,320,640,10, etc. (10, etc. because the next parlayed bet would have been 1280, exceeding the $1000 max bet limit).

It was arbitrarily decided that 320 and 640 bets at a $10 table were an unrealistic, impractical amount for a basic $10 bettor to consider using, so those bets were dropped from further consideration.

1, 2, 3, and 4-step WP parlays (no bailout) were tested, using the 31,658-hand spreadsheet.

The results ($10 table) were:

| WP bet sequence | $W/L | % of amt bet. |
|---|---|---|
| 1.  20,10, etc.------------------ | -2630-------- | -0.61 |
| 2.  20,40,10, etc.--------------- | -3380-------- | -0.62 |
| 3.  20,40,80,10, etc.------------ | -6425-------- | -0.97 |
| 4.  20,40,80,160,10, etc.--------- | -875-------- | -0.11 |

This means the least losing WP bet strategy (% of amt bet) is a sequence of 4 parlayed steps of bet increases.

For the above WP's, an improvement to the results was found, which is to delay a step in the WP bet sequence before starting the 4 step bet increases. This means, after winning a $10 bet, place another $10 bet before starting the WP progressive bet increases.

The results of this change are:

| WP bet sequence | $W/L | % of amt bet. |
|---|---|---|
| 1.  10,20,10, etc.---------------- | -1905-------- | -0.50 |
| 2.  10,20,40,10, etc.------------ | -3210-------- | -0.74 |
| 3.  10,20,40,80,10, etc.---------- | -620-------- | -0.13 |
| 4.  10,20,40,80,160,10, etc.------ | -1145-------- | -0.22 |

Even though results of #3 are slightly better than #4, #4 is the pattern of 4-step bet increases that will be used for WP bet strategies going forward.

But, since the 160 bet may be too salty for some players, a choice of 3 WP bet sequences with a lower top bet is added to the WP=20,40,80,160,10, etc. bet sequence. Proof tested results (no bailout) are listed.

| WP bet sequence | $W/L | % of amt bet. |
|---|---|---|
| 1. 10,20,40,45,50,10, etc.--------2055-------0.44 | | |
| 2. 10,20,40,70,75,10, etc.--------1218-------0.24 | | |
| 3. 10,20,40,80,100,10, etc.-------935--------0.18 | | |
| 4. 10,20,40,80,160,10, etc.------1145--------0.22 | | |

**Lose-Hand Progressions (LP)** bet strategies use the following routine:

- Increase the bet after a losing hand.
- Bet table minimum after a winning hand.

When using an LP bet strategy, "delay and up" as used in WP bet strategies, is not needed, so LP bet increases can start immediately after the first losing hand.

The same steps used for proof-testing WP progressions were used to proof-test LP progressions.

The results, no bailout strategy applied, were:

| WP bet sequence | $W/L | % of amt bet. |
|---|---|---|
| 1. 20,10, etc.----------------2885-----------0.66 | | |
| 2. 20,40,10, etc.-------------2225-----------0.39 | | |
| 3. 20,40,80,10, etc.---------+225-----------+0.03 | | |
| 4. 20,40,80,160,10, etc.---+2550---------- +0.30 | | |

This led to the same conclusion that the best winning LP bet strategy pattern is a sequence of 4 steps of bet increases.

So, a range of 4 LP's, with top bets ranging from 50 to 160 dollars (same as the 4 WP's), was selected and proof tested using the 31,658-hand spreadsheet. The results are for the LPs, no bailout.

| WP bet sequence | $W/L | % of amt. bet. |
|---|---|---|
| 1. 20,40,45,50,10, etc.------ | -380------------- | -0.06 |
| 2. 20,40,70,75,10, etc.------ | +883------------- | +0.12 |
| 3. 20,40,80,100,10, etc.--- | +1620------------- | +0.20 |
| 4. 20,40,80,160,10, etc.--- | +2550------------- | +0.30 |

# BAILOUT STRATEGY

There are numerous reasons to quit a blackjack session, some of which have nothing to do with winning or losing. Example:

- It's time to go to your room or go home.
- It's time for a meal or go to a show.
- Any other reason not related to blackjack.

These are labeled as "no bailout" in this book.

This book uses a 2-part bailout strategy. Quit betting and end the session if:

- During the latest losing streak in a session run, the # of losing hands exceed the # of winning hands by 4 or 5, (depending on your bet strategy).
- You have reached your Win Goal (WG) and then played on until losing a hand, then bailout.

A short cut label for the bailout strategy is: "**x:WG**".

Card counters do not use a bailout strategy. They play "shoe-to-shoe", starting over with the card counting bet strategy on the 1st hand after every reshuffle.

When using the bet/bailout strategies in this book, play "session-to-session".

A "session" always starts on the 1st hand after a reshuffle and ends after a bailout.

It can be as short as a couple of hands or as long as several shoes.

Instead of starting over with your bet strategy at the 1st hand after every reshuffle, continue with whatever size bet your bet strategy called for after the last hand of the previous round.

For example, after finishing the last hand of a shoe, if the next bet called for by your bet strategy is 40, place 40 as your 1st bet after the reshuffle.

If bailing out after a losing session, color up and leave the table.

If bailing out after a winning session, either sit out the rest of the hands in the shoe and start over after a reshuffle or color up and wait to start a new session later or the next time visiting a casino.

# BET/BAILOUT COMBINATIONS

This is where it all comes together. Specific bet strategies are described in the 31,658-hand spreadsheet. Then, each of the bailout strategies to go with each bet strategy are described and "cut and try" tested to find the best combination long run results.

| Bet Sequence | B/O Strategy | W/L $ |
|---|---|---|
| Flat Bet $10 | 4:40 | +975 |
| WP=10,20,40,45,50,10 etc. | 4:125 | +3165 |
| WP=10,20,40,70,75,10 etc. | 5:130 | +4428 |
| WP=10,20,40,80,100,10 etc. | 5:115 | +5470 |
| WP=10,20,40,80,160,10 etc. | 5:100 | +6325 |
| LP=20,40,45,50,10 etc. | 5:100 | +5020 |
| LP=20,40,70,75,10 etc. | 5:100 | +7070 |
| LP=20,40,80,100,10 etc. | 5:100 | +7635 |
| LP=20,40,80,160,10 etc. | 5:105 | +8935 |

Note that the best "x" bailout factor is 4 for the flat $10 and WP=10,20,40,45,50,10 etc. bet strategies. It is 5 for the remaining bet strategies.

The LP's show an advantage ranging from 69% to 138% in overall winnings compared to the WP's.

# CASE THE TABLE (RETRACTED)

In my previous book, "Blackjack Bailout A Winning System", I recommended a "Case the Table" routine to improve winning results, long run for LP bettors.

After devising a way to test the routine, I discovered the routine does the opposite, it slightly lowers winning results.

So, I am retracting the recommendation and apologize to those who may be using the routine.

There is no need to go into further detail.

# THE BAILOUT ADVANTAGE

The following chart compares the average before and after $ Won or Lost for a "no bailout" and then a "full bailout" strategy for all 9 bet/bailout strategies.

| Bet Sequence | -----------W/L $-------- | |
|---|---|---|
| | No B/O | Full B/O |
| Flat Bet $10-------------------------- | -1655 | +975 |
| WP=10,20,40,45,50,10 etc.--------- | -2055 | +3165 |
| WP=10,20,40,70,75,10 etc.---------- | -1218 | +4428 |
| WP=10,20,40,80,100,10 etc.-------- | -935 | +5470 |
| WP=10,20,40,80,160,10 etc.-------- | -1145 | +6325 |
| LP=20,40,45,50,10 etc.------------- | -380 | +5020 |
| LP=20,40,70,75,10 etc.------------ | +883 | +7070 |
| LP=20,40,80,100,10 etc.---------- | +1620 | +7635 |
| LP=20,40,80,160,10 etc.---------- | +2550 | +8935 |

A decision to use a full bailout strategy is a "no brainer".

Average W/L $, full bailout, are far better than for no bailout.

# SIMPLE TRAC

<u>Two situations</u> need to be tracked if using the bet/bailout strategies in this book.

1.  Progress toward reaching your Win Goal (WG).
2.  The excess of losing hands over winners in the most recent streak of hands.

We start with the setup when you first take a seat at the blackjack table.

<u>Buy-in</u>. The following chart lists the recommended buy-in $ at a $10 table for each of the 9 bet/bailout strategies in this book.

| <u>Bet Sequence</u> | <u>Buy-In $</u> |
|---|---|
| Flat Bet $10 | 100 |
| WP=10,20,40,45,50,10 etc. | 200 |
| WP=10,20,40,70,75,10 etc. | 200 |
| WP=10,20,40,80,100,10 etc. | 200 |
| WP=10,20,40,80,160,10 etc. | 300 |

LP=20,40,45,50,10 etc---------------300
LP=20,40,70,75,10 etc---------------300
LP=20,40,80,100,10 etc-------------400
LP=20,40,80,160,10 etc-------------500

The buy-in is split into 2 parts, a Bet Line (BL) and a Slush Fund.

The $ amounts for each are listed in the following chart, next page.

| Bet Sequence | Buy-In $ | Bet Line $ | Slush $ |
|---|---|---|---|
| Flat Bet $10------------------- | 100-------- | 60-------- | 40 |
| WP=10,20,40,45,50,10 etc.--- | 200------- | 135-------- | 65 |
| WP=10,20,40,70,75,10 etc.--- | 200------- | 135-------- | 65 |
| WP=10,20,40,80,100,10 etc.-- | 200------- | 150-------- | 50 |
| WP=10,20,40,80,160,10 etc.-- | 300------- | 195------- | 105 |
| LP=20,40,45,50,10 etc.-------- | 300------- | 210-------- | 90 |
| LP=20,40,70,75,10 etc.-------- | 300------- | 285-------- | 15 |
| LP=20,40,80,100,10 etc.------ | 400------- | 345-------- | 55 |
| LP=20,40,80,160,10 etc.------ | 500------- | 465-------- | 35 |

Use buy-in chips in a setup and routine to signal exactly when to bailout of a session after reaching your win goal (WG).

The total setup and the routine to use it is as illustrated.

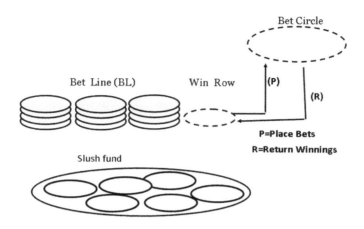

The Slush Fun amount is the difference between your buy-in and Bet Line (BL).

It is also the source of funds for anything not directly related to playing blackjack, such as making side bets, tips for the dealer or waitress, placing bets for the dealer or any other reason.

The Win Row and the Bet Line are the source of funds for placing a blackjack bet.

The Win Row keeps track of your progress toward reaching your win goal (WG).

The Bet Line is set up in 3 equally $ sized stacks of chips, for a grand total as shown on the following chart. It depends on your chosen bet strategy. NOte that it is a "full" amount. *Do not overfill during play.*

| Bet Sequence | ----Bet Line Setup---- | |
|---|---|---|
| | Full Amt | Each Stack |
| Flat Bet $10------------------------- 60------------ 20 | | |
| | | |
| WP=10,20,40,45,50,10 etc.---------- 135------------ 45 | | |
| WP=10,20,40,70,75,10 etc.---------- 135------------ 45 | | |
| WP=10,20,40,80,100,10 etc.--------- 150------------ 50 | | |
| WP=10,20,40,80,160,10 etc.--------- 195------------ 65 | | |
| | | |
| LP=20,40,45,50,10 etc.--------------- 210------------ 70 | | |
| LP=20,40,70,75,10 etc.-------------- 285------------ 95 | | |
| LP=20,40,80,100,10 etc.------------- 345------------ 115 | | |
| LP=20,40,80,160,10 etc.------------- 465------------ 155 | | |

Since most WG's for the WP & LP bet/bailout strategies in this book are in the vicinity of $100, it is suggested the Win Row stacks of chips be limited to $50 each.

When the Win Row reaches the Win Goal (WG), keep playing until losing a hand, then bailout.

Tracking excess losing hands. Use your off hand in your lap, under the table, to track the excess of losing hands over winners.

During play, the hand will either be a closed fist or with digits (thumb included) flipped open.

The general routine is to flip open digits after a losing hand or close open digits after a winning hand.

Flip open 1 digit after a losing hand or 2 digits after a double down losing hand.

Close 1 open digit after a winning hand or 2 open digits after a double down winning hand. Obviously, when there are no open digits, you do nothing.

Make no change after a push hand.

If using flat betting $10 or WP=10,20,40,45,50,10 etc. bet/bailout strategy, bailout if you reach 4 open digits.

If using any other bet/bailout strategy, bailout if you reach 5 open digits.

# TRACK THE RUNNING TOTAL

A friend may ask "How are you doing playing blackjack?".

You may ask yourself, "How am I doing?".

You'll need to track your running total in the long run to truthfully answer either question.

If you don't keep track, you'll be prone to answer based on the results of your most recent session(s). This can be misleading.

Using the LP=20,40,80,100,10 etc. bet/bailout strategy as an example, the maximum win session for the 31,658-hand spreadsheet run was $240. The maximum loss session was -$360.

The *average* result was winning $5.81 per session.

So, the *average* win or loss per session is the key # to look for as you track the running total.

Get a 3x5 notepad and prepare the 1st page in the format as illustrated, next page.

| SES'N # | AMT W/L | RUN TOT'L | AVG W or L PER SES'N |
|---|---|---|---|
| 1 | | | |
| 2 | | | |
| 3 | | | |
| 4 | | | |
| 5 | | | |
| 6 | | | |
| 7 | | | |
| 8 | | | |
| 9 | | | |
| 10 | | | |
| 11 | | | |
| 12 | | | |
| 13 | | | |
| 14 | | | |
| 15 | | | |

Take the notebook and a pen or pencil with you to the blackjack table.

After bailing out and finishing a session, write the $ amount won or lost in the 1st column.

Compute and fill in the run total and avg W or L columns at your convenience after going home or back to your room.

The run total is the sum of the previous session run total and the current session amount w/l.

The average W or L per session is the run total divided by the session #.

By following this routine you'll always know where you stand compared to the long run average.

# SCALING UP THE BET LEVEL

At this point, a range of 9 different bet/bailout strategies, along with their proven long run results, have been revealed for use at a $10 minimum bet table.

But, if there are no $10 tables available or you simply just choose to play at a $15 minimum bet table, you'll need to scale up your bet/bailout strategy numbers, as follows:

- Except for "x" in the bailout strategy, multiply each of the other numbers in the $10 bet/bailout strategy by 1.5 and round up any number, if necessary, to an even $5 increment.

For example, the LP=20,40,80,100,10etc., 5:100 bet/bailout strategy used at a $10 table scales up to LP=30,60,120,150,15 etc., 5:150 at a $15 table.

The buy-in and Bet Line (BL) numbers also scale up to $600 and $525 (rounded up) respectively.

The W/L results scale up to $11,453, but the % of amount bet remains the same at +1.57.

The scale up factor for a $25 table 2.5. I leave it to the reader to do the math, in a manner as described above.

Same as for a $100 table, where the scale up factor is 10.

# RECAP

As part of the final chapter, the last page of this book displays the basic playing strategy crib card which is free to cut out or copy for your personal use.

A unique feature of this book was the creation of a 31,658-hand spreadsheet to "proof-test" various non-card counting bet/bailout strategies for long run results.

The big advantage of the spreadsheet run is that it uses the same run of blackjack hands to compare the result of different bet/bailout strategies.

In my humble opinion, using the same results qualify the 31,658-hand spreadsheet run as a legitimate "long run".

The comparisons are true apples-to-apples, not a different run vs. another as used by card counters.

The "Bet/Bailout Combinations" chapter summarizes the results of $10 flat betting and 8 different progression bet/bailout strategies, all 9 of which were proven to be long run winners by the 31,658-hand spreadsheet run.

The bet system examples in this book are simple and straightforward. Your choice is easy to remember for use at the table.

A simple way to track when to bailout was provided, essential to getting a long run winning result.

Also, a format was provided, to use with a 3x5 notebook, to track your running win or loss $ total.

Finally, a way to scale up your bet level was described.

As promised, the basic playing strategy crib card is displayed, free to be cut out or copied and used at the blackjack table. When you sit down to play, be sure to show it to the dealer and ask for permission to use it at the table. I have never been refused.

| | Playr Hand | 2 | 3 | 4 | 5 | 6 | 7 | 8 | 9 | 10 | A |
|---|---|---|---|---|---|---|---|---|---|---|---|
| | | **BASIC PLAYING STRATEGY** | | | | | | | | | |
| | | | | — Dealer Up-Card — | | | | | | | |
| H | 5-8 | Always Hit | | | | | | | | | |
| H | 9 | Hit | Dbl Dwn | | | | Hit | | | | |
| a | 10 | Dbl Dwn | | | | | | | | Hit | |
| r | 11 | Dbl Dwn | | | | | | | | | Hit |
| d | 12 | Hit | | Stand | | | Hit | | | | |
| | 13-16 | Stand | | | | | Hit | | | | |
| | 17-21 | Always Stand | | | | | | | | | |
| S | A,8-10 | Always Stand | | | | | | | | | |
| o | A,2-3 | Hit | | DD | | | Hit | | | | |
| f | A,4-5 | Hit | | Dbl Dwn | | | Hit | | | | |
| t | A,6 | Hit | Dbl Dwn | | | | Hit | | | | |
| | A,7 | Std | Dbl Dwn | | | | Stand | | Hit | | |
| | | 2 | 3 | 4 | 5 | 6 | 7 | 8 | 9 | 10 | A |
| | 2's,3's, | Split | | | | | Hit | | | | |
| P | 4's | Hit | | Split | | | Hit | | | | |
| a | 5's | Dbl Dwn | | | | | | | | Hit | |
| i | 6's | Split | | | | | Hit | | | | |
| r | 7's | Split | | | | | Hit | | | | |
| s | 8's, A's | Always Split | | | | | | | | | |
| | 9's | Split | | | | | Std | Split | | Stand | |
| | 10's | Always Stand | | | | | | | | | |